SMART W READER

VOLCANOES

Judith Bauer Stamper

SCHOLASTIC INC.
New York Toronto London Auckland
Sydney Mexico City New Delhi Hong Kong

What are SMART WORDS?

Smart Words are frequently-used words that are critical to understanding concepts taught in the classroom. The more Smart Words a child knows, the more easily he or she will grasp important curriculum concepts. Smart Words readers introduce these key words in a fun and motivational format while developing important literacy skills. Each new word is highlighted, defined in context, and reviewed. Engaging activities at the end of each chapter allow readers to practice the words they have learned.

ISBN 978-0-545-28543-8

Packaged by Q2AMedia

Copyright © 2010 by Scholastic Inc.

Photo credits: t= top, b= bottom, l= left, r= right

Cover Page: Corey Ford/123RF, Bychkov Kirill Alexandrovich/Shutterstock.
Title Page: Bychkov Kirill Alexandrovich/Shutterstock.
Content Page: Juliengrondin/Shutterstock.

4-5: Austin Post/U.S. Geological Survey; 5: James Steidl/Istockphoto; 6-7: D.W. Peterson/U.S. Geological Survey; 7: J.D. Griggs/U.S. Geological Survey; 8-9: Bychkov Kirill Alexandrovich/Shutterstock; 9: R.S. Culbreth, U.S. Air Force/U.S. Geological Survey; 11t: Glen Petitpas 2004; 11c: U.S. Geological Survey; 11b: Lyn Topinka/U.S. Geological Survey; 12: Juliengrondin/Shutterstock; 13: Guenter Guni/Istockphoto; 16: Corey Ford/123RF; 18: Iofoto/Shutterstock; 20-21: C. Stoughton/U.S. Geological Survey; 22: Dhuss/Istockphoto; 23: Michael Gray/Istockphoto; 24-25: Austin Post/U.S. Geological Survey; 26-27: R.L. Christiansen/U.S. Geological Survey; 28-29: S Jonasson/FLPA; 30-31: Juliengrondin/Shutterstock; 32: Warren Goldswain/Shutterstock.

Q2AMedia Art Bank: 10, 14-15, 17, 19, 24.

All rights reserved. Published by Scholastic Inc.

SCHOLASTIC and associated logos are trademarks and/or registered trademarks of Scholastic Inc.

22 21 20 19   14 15/0

Printed in the U.S.A.   40
First printing, September 2010

Table of Contents

Chapter 1

When Earth Explodes

First, there is a rumble. Then, there is a BOOM. A **volcano** is blowing its top!

A volcano is an opening in the Earth's surface. When it **erupts**, the volcano shoots out melted rock, ash, and gases. It looks like the Earth is exploding.

BOOM!

Mount St. Helens blew its top in 1980.

There are over 1,500 active volcanoes in the world. An active volcano can erupt at any time. For people living nearby, that could be bad news.

Mount Etna in Italy is a huge, fiery volcano.

SMART WORDS

volcano   an opening in Earth's surface. Melted rock, ash, and gases escape through it

erupt   to spew out melted rock, ash, and gases

Some volcanoes shoot out **lava**, melted rock from inside the Earth. The lava may ooze slowly out of the volcano. Or it may explode out like fireworks.

Lava is red-hot! It can measure up to 2,282 degrees Fahrenheit (1,250 degrees Celsius). A lava flow looks like a river of fire. It destroys everything in its path.

A fiery river of lava flows down Mount Kilauea in Hawaii.

As the lava cools, it turns from a red liquid to a black solid. Two types of lava get their names from Hawaiian words.

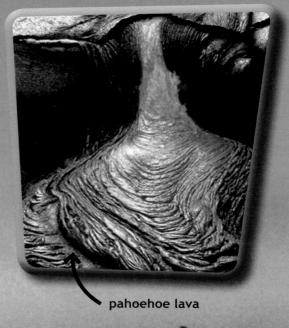

pahoehoe lava

Pahoehoe lava cools to form a smooth rock. It has a ropy pattern on its surface.

A'a lava cools to form a sharp, rough rock. It is painful to walk on!

SMART WORDS

lava hot melted rock that erupts from a volcano and reaches Earth's surface

Some volcanoes erupt with a blast of **ash** and **gas**. Huge grey clouds of ash explode out of the volcano. The ash is mixed with hot, poisonous gases.

This type of eruption is more deadly than a lava flow. The ash and gas clouds can travel as fast as 99 miles (160 kilometers) per hour. Anyone caught in these clouds has little chance of surviving.

A huge cloud of ash and gases rises from Karimsky Volcano in Russia.

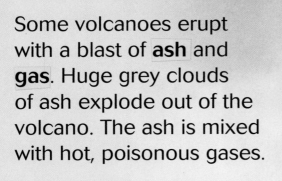

The volcanic ash falls down and covers everything for miles around. It looks like a soft grey blanket, but it is very dangerous.

The ash can choke plants and trees. It can bury houses and cars. It can even block the sun and make a **climate** cooler.

People flee the clouds of ash from Mount Pinatubo in the Philippines.

SMART WORDS

ash dust-sized rock material that blows out of a volcano

gas a substance that will spread to fill any space that contains it

climate the usual weather in a place

Volcanoes have different shapes and are formed in different ways.

Volcano Type	Description
 **Shield Volcano**	A shield volcano is wider than it is high. It is made of lava that flows out rather than explodes. It is so wide because the thin, runny lava travels farther before it hardens.
 **Cinder Cone Volcano**	A cinder cone volcano looks like a cone-shaped hill. It is made of layers of cinders and ash that build up after eruptions. A cinder cone often has a bowl-shaped pit on top called a **crater**. It forms after a big explosion blows off the volcano's top.
 **Composite Volcano**	A composite volcano looks like a tall mountain with steep sides. It is made of alternating layers of lava and ash. It is high and steep because its thick lava does not travel far before it hardens. This volcano can have a crater as well.

Mauna Loa in Hawaii is a shield volcano.

Paricutin in Mexico is a cinder cone volcano. A deep crater tops it.

Mount Shasta in California is a composite volcano.

Use your SMART WORDS

Point to the Smart Word that matches each description.

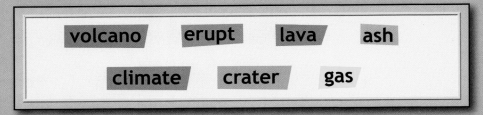

volcano	erupt	lava	ash
climate	crater	gas	

1. It is an opening in the Earth's surface. Lava, ash, and gases escape through it.
2. It is melted rock from a volcano.
3. It is what a volcano does when it spews out lava, ash, and gases.
4. It is the usual weather of a place.
5. It is dust-sized rock from a volcano.
6. It is a substance that will spread to fill any space that contains it.
7. It is a bowl-shaped pit at the top of a volcano.

Answers on page 32

Talk Like a Scientist

What's happening in this picture?
Use Smart Words to talk about it.

SMART FACTS

Did You Know?

There are at least 1,500 active volcanoes around the world. About 500 million people live near them!

That's Amazing!

The lava flow from most volcanoes is thick and slow-moving. The lava from Mount Nyiragongo in Africa flows much faster. In 1977, the volcano erupted. The hot lava raced down the mountain at 60 miles (96 kilometers) per hour! Many people living in nearby villages could not escape in time.

How Big?

Mount Nyiragongo has a crater that is 1.3 miles (2 kilometers) wide and 820 feet (250 meters) deep. The crater is usually filled with hot, liquid lava.

Chapter 2
INSIDE THE Earth

What makes a volcano erupt? Deep inside Earth, **temperatures** are so high that rock melts into a hot liquid called **magma**. The magma rises up and collects in large pools called magma chambers.

Pressure pushes the magma up toward Earth's surface. The magma rises up through a tube, or **vent**, inside the volcano. The pressure on the magma gets stronger and stronger.

Finally, the volcano erupts! When the magma shoots out of the volcano, it is called lava.

SMART WORDS

temperature   the degree of hotness or coldness

magma   hot liquid rock deep inside the Earth

pressure   the force exerted by pressing on something

vent   the opening of a volcano through which lava, ash, and gases escape

magma

magma chamber

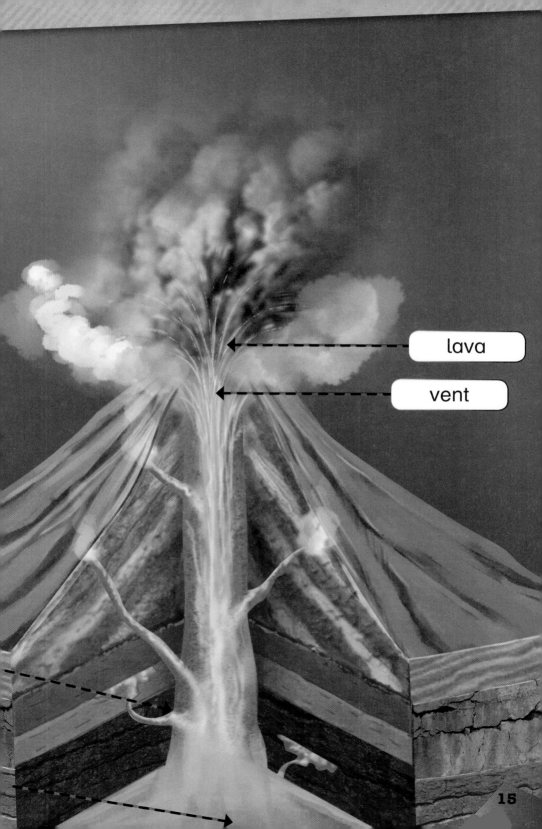

lava

vent

The Ring of Fire is a belt of active volcanoes around the Pacific Ocean. The ring outlines the edges of a **tectonic plate**, a large piece of Earth's **crust**. Many volcanic eruptions happen where the Earth's plates meet.

Earth's tectonic plates move and grind against each other with great force. One plate gets pushed deeper inside Earth. The hot temperature there melts it into magma. Pressure pushes the magma up to the Earth's surface. All this activity inside Earth causes volcanoes to erupt around the Ring of Fire.

There are 452 volcanoes located in the Ring of Fire. That includes over one-half of the world's active volcanoes!

SMART WORDS

tectonic plate   a large, movable piece of Earth's crust

crust   the hard outer layer of Earth

The Ring of Fire

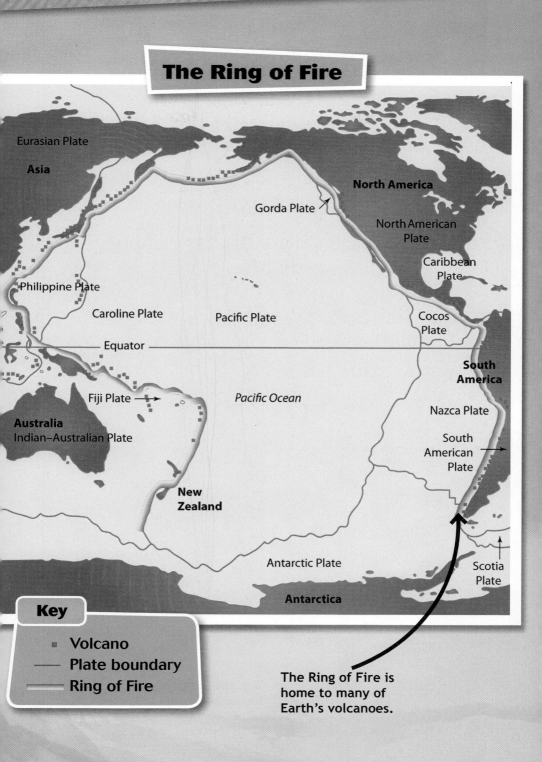

Eurasian Plate

Asia

North America

Gorda Plate

North American Plate

Caribbean Plate

Philippine Plate

Caroline Plate

Pacific Plate

Cocos Plate

Equator

South America

Fiji Plate

Pacific Ocean

Nazca Plate

Australia
Indian–Australian Plate

South American Plate

New Zealand

Antarctic Plate

Scotia Plate

Antarctica

Key

- ■ Volcano
- —— Plate boundary
- —— Ring of Fire

The Ring of Fire is home to many of Earth's volcanoes.

Hawaii is home to two of the biggest volcanoes on Earth, Mauna Loa and Kilauea. These volcanoes sit on top of a **hot spot**. A hot spot lies above an extremely hot area of magma under the Earth's crust. Hot spots are in the middle of tectonic plates, not at the edges.

The Hawaiian Islands are the tips of huge underwater mountains. They were formed by the build-up of lava over millions of years. The Hawaiian hot spot does not move. The tectonic plate above it does. Each Hawaiian island formed as it sat over the hot spot.

The island of Hawaii has several black sand beaches. The sand is made of small pieces of lava.

A new volcano named Loihi is growing below the sea to the south. Loihi rises 9,843 feet (3,000 meters) from the ocean floor. However, its peak is still far below the ocean surface. Someday, Loihi will be the newest Hawaiian island.

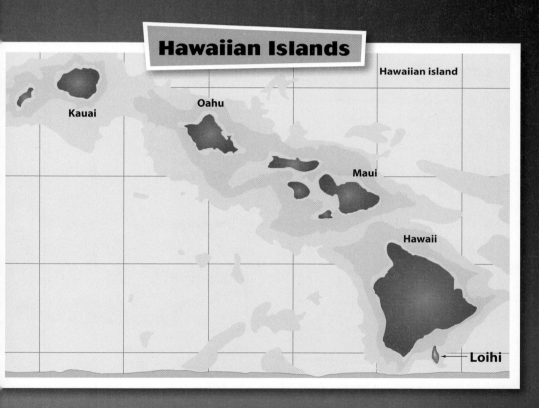

Hawaiian Islands

Hawaiian island

Kauai

Oahu

Maui

Hawaii

Loihi

SMART WORDS

hot spot   a place that lies above an extremely hot area of magma under the Earth's crust

Use your SMART WORDS

Read each description. Use a Smart Word to name what it tells about.

magma	temperature	pressure
tectonic plate	hot spot	crust	vent

1. the hard outer layer of Earth

2. a place that lies above an extremely hot area of magma under Earth's crust

3. a big piece of Earth's crust

4. the opening of a volcano through which lava, ash, and gases escape

5. melted rock below the surface of the Earth

6. the degree of hotness or coldness

7. the force exerted by pressing on something

Answers on page 32

Talk Like a Scientist

Would you want to live near the Ring of Fire? Why or why not? Explain your answer using Smart Words.

SMART FACTS

Did You Know?

Pele is the volcano goddess of Hawaiian legend. The legend says that Pele lives in the crater of Kilauea. When tourists visit Hawaii, they are warned about Pele's curse: Bad luck will come to anyone who takes rocks away from the islands.

Record Breaker

Kazumura Cave on the big island of Hawaii is the longest lava tube in the world. It is 41 miles (66 kilometers) long! A lava tube is a cave that runs through a hardened lava flow.

The crater of Kilauea

That's Amazing!

Hawaii has plenty of sharp lava rock that they call a'a. An old story says the name a'a came from the sound a person would make when walking barefoot across the lava.

Chapter 3

Disaster Watch

Volcanoes are dangerous and deadly. They can erupt with little warning. For people living nearby, an eruption can be a **disaster**!

In 79 AD, Mount Vesuvius in Italy erupted. The people of Pompeii lived near the volcano. They didn't have time to escape. Some died from the eruption's intense heat. Others were killed by ash and gas.

Pompeii itself was buried under many feet of ash. Centuries later, scientists dug out the buried town. Today, visitors can see plaster casts of the victims, caught at their moment of death.

These are plaster casts of volcano victims in Pompeii.

Mt. St. Helens is located in Washington.

A volcano disaster struck the United States in 1980. Mount St. Helens in Washington had been quiet for 123 years. Two months before it erupted, the volcano showed signs of activity. Scientists watched the volcano carefully. However, no one **predicted** what would happen on May 18, 1980.

With a huge explosion, Mount St. Helens blew its top. One side of the mountain was ripped off. Lava poured down its slopes. Clouds of ash filled the air.

Lava, rocks, ash, and mud buried everything up to 7 miles (27 kilometers) away. It destroyed acres of forests and millions of animals. Fifty-seven people did not have time to **evacuate** the area. They could not outrun the volcano's violence.

predict   to say what will happen in the future

evacuate   to move away from a dangerous area

How can we stay safe from disaster? Scientists called **volcanologists** study volcanoes. They use special tools to **measure** a volcano's activity.

Volcanologists take photos from helicopters and satellites. They listen for rumblings inside the Earth. They measure changing temperatures. Sometimes, volcanologists go inside a volcano's crater to **observe** it up close!

This volcanologist wears a special heat suit to study a volcano.

Volcanologists watch for signs that a volcano might erupt. If a volcano looks dangerous, they alert people who live nearby. An early warning can save thousands of lives.

Science can keep us safer from volcanic eruptions. However, it can never stop them.

Volcanoes are nature's power, unleashed!

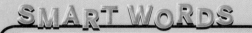

SMART WORDS

volcanologist   a scientist who studies volcanoes

measure   to find out the size, weight, etc. of something

observe   to watch someone or something carefully

Answer each question with the correct Smart Word.

disaster	evacuate	measure
volcanologist	observe	predict

1. What kind of scientist studies volcanoes?

2. What do you do if you move away from a dangerous area?

3. How do you watch someone or something carefully?

4. What is an event that causes great damage, loss, or suffering?

5. What do you do if you say what you think will happen in the future?

6. How do you find out the size, weight, etc. of something?

Answers on page 32

Talk Like a Scientist

What questions would you ask a volcanologist? Ask two questions using Smart Words.

SMART FACTS

Did You Know?

The word *volcano* comes from Vulcan, the Roman god of fire. The Romans believed that Vulcan had his fiery forge inside a volcano.

About That Word

The word *volcanologist* has two parts. One is *volcan–*. The other is *–ologist*. This ending means "a person who studies."

The island of Surtsey.

That's Amazing!

In 1963, Earth got a new island. An underwater volcano erupted near Iceland. Lava built up until the island emerged from the water. The island takes its name from Surtur, a giant of fire in Icelandic myths. It is called Surtsey.

Glossary

ash   dust-sized rock material that blows out of a volcano

climate   the usual weather in a place

crater   a bowl-shaped pit at the top of a volcano

crust   the hard outer layer of Earth

disaster   an event that causes great damage, loss, or suffering

erupt   to become active and spew out melted rock and ash

evacuate   to move away from a dangerous area

gas   a substance that will spread to fill any space that contains it

hot spot   a place that lies above an extremely hot area of magma under the Earth's crust

lava   hot melted rock that erupts from a volcano and reaches Earth's surface

magma melted rock below the surface of Earth

measure to find out the size, weight, etc. of something

observe to watch someone or something carefully

predict to say what you think will happen in the future

pressure the force exerted by pressing on something

tectonic plate a large piece of Earth's crust that moves over the mantle

temperature the degree of hotness or coldness

vent the opening of a volcano through which lava, ash, and gases escape

volcano an opening in Earth's surface. Melted rock, ash, and gases escape through it.

volcanologist a scientist who studies volcanoes

Index

SMART WORDS Answer Key

Page 12
1. volcano, 2. lava, 3. erupt, 4. climate, 5. ash, 6. gas, 7. crater

Page 20
1. crust, 2. hot spot, 3. tectonic plate, 4. vent, 5. magma, 6. temperature, 7. pressure

Page 28
1. volcanologist, 2. evacuate, 3. observe, 4. disaster 5. predict, 6. measure